You Want It?
Then Damn It,
Go & Get It!
An Inspirational Roadmap For Personal Productivity

To mary
love, Renée

Renée Armand

Published by: SkyLight Creative
Edited by: Michelle Abrams
Copyright 2016 Renée Armand

ISBN-10: 0692570640
ISBN-13: 978-0-692-57064-7

DEDICATION

This book is dedicated with love to Ma and Dad.
One helped me stay secure and well grounded,
while the other taught me how to soar. I got the best
of both worlds.

...

*"The secret of getting ahead is getting started. The
secret of getting started is breaking your complex
overwhelming tasks into small manageable tasks,
and then starting on the first one."*
– Mark Twain.

CONTENTS

PART I

PART II

ACKNOWLEDGMENTS

I would like to give special thanks to Ann and Raymond St.Cyr, Michelle Abrams, Brenda O'Connor, Janice Fennelly and Angie Papadopolous. You each took the time to read this book while it was in the works and your advice and encouragement has meant the world to me. Thank you for being the special people you are and for making a difference.

HOW TO USE THIS BOOK

This book has been written like a roadmap. It takes you in a sequential manner from where you are to where you want to be. At times however, you may not find the whole process is needed. For this reason it is sectioned out, so feel free to pick and chose what is helpful to you.

Throughout the book, it will be suggested that you take some type of action. This will be explained, but also identified by a plus sign (+). As a reader of self-help books, there are times when it may be uncertain if what is being explained will come again, or if you should be diving in and taking action at that particular moment. I want you to immerse yourself in the reading and not worry about taking notes or wondering if you've missed something along the way.

So many people live their lives day in and day out, doing the same thing, riding the same train, going to the same job they are perhaps miserable at, feeling stuck. Because you are reading this book, I know you've woken up! For some inexplicable reason, the veil has been removed from your eyes and you're like Dorothy, opening up the door to Oz for the first time in its entire Technicolor splendor.

Life is a journey. You'll complete something, learn from the experience and get ready to move onto the next road to travel in your life. I encourage you to enjoy and appreciate the journey as much as the finish line.

You Want It? Then Damn It, Go & Get It!

1 IT ENDS AND BEGINS

IT was December 2, 2008 at 9:20 a.m. I was in my office at an asset management firm in Boston, where I had just spent close to 20 years of my life. I joined the firm just out of college, beginning my career as an administrative assistant, working my way up the corporate ladder to level of vice president within the Marketing Department.

The phone rang that morning and I was asked by the director of Marketing to come to her office. She had something she wanted to discuss. At the time, it didn't seem odd, as I knew restructuring was in the works, and I honestly thought she wanted some input.

Minutes after the meeting, I was walking in a daze to Human Resources. I was being let go, along with a considerable number of other co-workers. This volatile time is now referred to as the financial crisis of 2008. In the U.S. alone, 2.6 million

jobs where lost that year, with many more to follow in its wake.

Within seconds, my world had turned upside down. I had the rest of the week to get my affairs in order. Walking back to my office and numb from what had just happened, I went back to work. In the middle of writing up a status report, I suddenly thought, "What the hell am I doing?"

I grabbed my coat and headed for the door, walked around some and ended up on a park bench. I sat there watching the people bustling around me. They all seemed to have somewhere to go. I felt invisible and disconnected. I finally phoned who was now suddenly my former boss, a man I reported to for well over 10 years. Before saying anything other than a weak hello, he said, "I guess you heard the news." I asked, "What news?" He said he had just been laid off. I paused for a moment and then I said, "So was I." His response was, "Are you fu*c%ing kidding me!?"

He asked where I was and I told him I'd left the office. He was still there and said word was starting to spread and everyone was a wreck. People were getting called throughout the firm. He suggested we meet at Kitty O'Shea's, a local watering hole, to regroup. He would let others know to meet us there.

People started pouring in to the bar. There were those who had already received the news we were being let go. Others were coming in and out all day, still concerned for themselves while offering condolences. We sat there from late morning until nightfall trying to comfort each other and make sense of what had just happened. Many of us later referred to it as the Day of the Irish Wake.

I recently went out with some close friends. We were talking about falling on hard times, and one girlfriend's comment was simple and perfect. She said, "When times are tough, that's when we do our best work. We hold each other together." Well, let me tell you, that was one of the toughest days of my life and, by God, we did our best work.

"The ultimate measure of a man is not where he stands in moments of comfort and convenience, but where he stands at times of challenge and controversy."
– Martin Luther King

A New Beginning

Confronted with a change as big as this, I had to make some decisions on where life was now going to take me. I had a supportive husband who was on board with letting me explore out-of-the-box options. I also knew I wanted to spend more time with my two young sons.

Throughout my career, I realized that success had to do with a number of factors, but I continued to see a reoccurring theme with the areas of attitude, communication, process and management. Be it people or projects, the process was pretty much the same, and frame of mind could easily make or break a project.

As part of my job, I traveled the world over many times to set up publishing teams and to ensure the needs of our internal clients were being met. I had learned so many skills in the business world, and how to apply them to other areas of my life.

I took on some fun and fulfilling challenges. One was the creation of a record label. I then went on to create *Time* (reneestcyr.com), an album of original songs (I released it under my maiden name, Renée St. Cyr). All of the writing and recording was done in my home studio and online with other collaborators.

During this time, a connection began to emerge somewhere between project management and personal productivity.

The world of project management focuses on the planning, organizing, managing, leading, and controlling of resources to achieve particular goals.

This is typically done with a team of people.

Personal productivity uses a lot of the same methodology as corporate project management, however you are now planning and organizing, and managing, leading and controlling resources for yourself and for the most part by yourself. I was using a number of techniques that I learned in a professional setting, which now came naturally to me. With the album complete, I began to see other areas where my skills might lead to other opportunities.

Next came SkyLight Creative, where I partnered with a local businesswoman to start a business focused on digital and innovative marketing solutions. Again, I learned the project management methods I used in the corporate world and in creating the album were put to good use with the new business. Not long after that, The Passion to Pursue (reneearmand.com) came along. This was an endeavor that was founded to help individuals overcome obstacles that prevent them from reaching their goals. I like to say it's where project management meets inspiration.

I began to see how this process could be used on just about anything I needed to get done, and I thought, why the heck wasn't I sharing this knowledge with others?

I recently woke from a sound sleep and saw that it was 3:00 a.m. The idea for this book was taunting me, daring me to write it. I grabbed my iPhone, opened my Notes application and started writing. When I looked up, it was 11:00 a.m. Hours had passed without me being aware of it. By then I had completed the outline for this book and was well on my way.

It's amazing to lose oneself in something that is meaningful. The feeling I got about writing this book is the same one that comes over me when a song takes hold. If it's a song that's meant to be written, there's pretty much no way of stopping it. Some other part of me takes over and I'm just an observer watching it all unfold.

In this book, I want to help you find that same experience, where you're able to immerse in something truly meaningful and watch it unfold.

2 GO & GET IT! METHOD

IT'S always good to know what you're getting into. This chapter gives a snapshot of what you'll set out to accomplish.

The premise of this book focuses on the Go & Get It! Method. This is a process that identifies a goal and paves the way to reach it.

Pretty much anything you want to do can be broken down into manageable steps. Whether it's taking a camping trip or traveling the world, once you've nailed the principles you can apply the same process to get from here to just about anywhere else.

In the following chapters, you will work on coming up with a Go & Get It! Method List, which will contain the specifics about what you would like to pursue.

From there, you will figure out the order of what you'd like to tackle first, second, third, and so on.

You'll then develop a mission statement, determine action items and devise a clear, concise approach for developing a personal roadmap, which will be your Go & Get It! Plan.

You'll also explore some potential hurdles that may be keeping you from your goals, as well as a few stories along the way to help keep you motivated.

My job is to take you through the process step-by-step, so it doesn't become overwhelming. Have you ever tried to get back into working out after avoiding it for a while? You're filled with exuberance and energy; you're fired up! You get a gym membership and kick in. Day one, you feel great! Day two, you're sore, but you're going to stick with it. By day three, you're super tired, but you're still going to make it to that gym no matter what. And so it goes. Before you know it, though, you're starting to lose steam because you've pushed yourself too hard and too fast. Yes, you will have to work for what you get, but I want you to avoid jumping in full force. The excitement and passion can and should be there. Let's just make sure you have a solid plan that's broken down into manageable pieces.

Go & Get It! **List** + Go & Get It! **Plan** = Go & Get It! **Method**

3 PROJECTS

"**WHY** do you have to make everything into a project?" Have you ever heard that saying? Umm, maybe because everything pretty much is? Seriously, think about it. Cleaning the house, making dinner, planning for that trip you've been putting off for years, or even teaching your children how to tie their sneakers: everything is a project be it small, medium, large or super-sized.

Some things you can just do because you're on autopilot: they flow easily because you've been doing them forever. A good example is getting ready in the morning. Do you know how many steps are actually involved with this process?

Years ago, I became certified to teach elementary school. One of the things that stuck with me most was how children acquired the skills to perform consecutive tasks. If you've ever had children of your own, there may have been a time or two where extra, extra, (ok, one more extra) patience was needed, especially during the morning rush of getting everyone out the door.

For example, I would tell my younger son, "Mikey, please finish up your cereal, put your dirty dishes in the dishwasher, head on upstairs and brush your teeth, get your socks and sneakers on, gather up your homework and your lunch and have a great day!" Yeah, right. In the early years, we'd be lucky to get through half of those tasks without me having to say it over and over again. It wasn't Mike's fault that he couldn't remember all the actions, as his cognitive skills were still developing.

As he and the rest of us continue to mature, these tasks become second nature. If it were only so easy for everything else in our lives we'd like to get done. Well, I'm here to tell you it can be. You have the power to go from here to there. Planning, holding yourself accountable, and having the right kind of attitude are what you really need. I'll help you get your dishes put away, teeth brushed, lunch and homework in hand, and out the door! First, let's get some potential obstacles out of the way.

4 IT'S ALL IN YOUR HEAD

"IT'S all in your head." You've all heard it. My answer to that is, "Well, of course it is!" When you're working toward a goal, just thinking about it may actually help improve your chances of success. This is called visualization. There are other names and methods for it. Guided imagery is done with a practitioner who helps to guide you through images in your mind. Neurolinguistic programming involves changing behavior patterns through the retraining of the mind. Autogenic training uses meditative techniques to relax the body in times of stress.

Ball In Motion

In the 1920s, Dr. Judd Blaslotto conducted a study at the University of Chicago on three groups of basketball players. The goal was to see how many free throw shots they could make. For 20 days straight, the first group practiced free throws every day for an hour, the second was asked to visualize throwing free throws, and the third group didn't do anything at all.

At the end of the study, the group that practiced improved by 24%. The group that visualized improved by 23%, and the group that didn't practice showed no improvement. Imagine (literally!) getting better at something just by thinking it?

A few years back, I was out with a group of friends. We went to a bowling alley in Boston. There were quite a few of us and we started breaking off into teams. As we were waiting our turn, I began chatting with a friend who was telling me how horrible she was at bowling. Out of curiosity, I asked her what she thought about as she was throwing the ball down the lane. She looked at me kind of funny for a second and then said, "I picture the ball flying into the gutter before it can even come close to hitting the pins." I asked if she would try a little experiment with me. I said, "The next time it's your turn, take a minute to visualize the ball in your hand, the lane, and the pins. Think of releasing the ball, only this time, envision the ball being thrown straight down the middle and all the pins toppling over."

When she was up next, she did just that. Where others may have seen something that resembled hesitation, I knew she was visualizing the scene. She picked up the ball, took a few steps down the lane, released the ball and watched as it went right down the middle and seconds later every last pin came a tumbling down. She turned around and caught my eye with a big smile on her face. She came running over and asked what I did. I told her I didn't do anything. She did it! And she continued to visualize and knock the pins down over and over again through the rest of the day.

Flying High

I had the privilege to see things first hand at an air show with a pilot named Buick (aviator call sign) who had been flying with the Black Diamond Jet Team. We were standing out on the tarmac, next to a Czech-designed L-39 Albatros single-engine jet before the show began.

There was a group of us chatting, and I realized Buick was no longer among us. I looked behind the jet and I saw him doing something that at first glance looked similar to Tai Chi. His body was flowing forward, backward, and sideways. His arms were making circular motions, and his full focus was completely inward. It was really amazing to watch.

After the spectacular air show, I asked about what I had seen him doing earlier. Buick said he had to go through the whole sequence of flying in his mind before he took flight. He pictured each dive, turn, and roll. The mental preparation was just as important as the physical act.

So how is this relevant to what you want to accomplish? Visualizing what you want and where you need to be helps you stay on target to reach your goals. Later in the book, I'll provide some helpful steps on how to go about visualization.

5 HERE & NOW

A crucial key to achieving your goals is learning how to avoid being sidetracked. One great way to stay on task is being able to stay in the moment. Some years ago, my husband received a book called, *The Present*, written by Spencer Johnson. It's a short, powerful, easy read and I highly recommend it. The premise is to learn from the past, remain in the present, and plan for the future.

Being focused on what is in the here and now really helps to keep you on track. And best of all, it quiets that "nervous Nellie" voice we all have in our heads. When you're in the present, you're focused and you don't have time to listen to the hubbub.

The first time I put it to use, I was in my car racing to work. I was running late for a meeting and I knew I'd be stuck in traffic. "Nellie" was egging me on to become more and more nervous. She chattered away about all the people who would be sitting around the conference room table waiting for me to arrive.

I had recently finished reading *The Present*, and for the first time I can recall, I caught myself and actually became aware of this negative inner voice. Even better, I realized I could quiet it! I said out loud, "Hey, shut up!" It was like magic. All of a sudden, I started to become aware of the tall, green cornstalks to the right and the red barn being built at the farm I passed every single day without really actually seeing it.

I put the window down and breathed in the fresh hay, felt the warm breeze on my face and noticed the chickens running around. I couldn't believe I had been missing out on this precious gift every single day.

There was absolutely nothing more I could do other than make a quick (hands-free) call to say I was running late. My co-workers had my meeting agenda, I asked someone else to lead, and that was that. The tension eased and I felt a weight lift from my shoulders. The circumstances didn't change; my attitude did. I shifted to the here and now. Whoa! How cool was that! I realized that day that I was separate from the nervous thoughts, and once I came to understand that, I knew I was the one who could control my emotions and my situation.

Even after losing my job the ability to stay in the present, as hard as it was, ended up being the best thing for me. It was important not to hide from what was happening. I felt the pain, gave myself reasonable time to grieve, and then moved on and thrived, knowing that this too shall pass. And sure, the pain still bubbles up once in awhile (especially since I worked in one of the most iconic buildings in

Boston that seems to pop up on the background set of every Boston news

cast or constant aerial shots on Boston based television shows), but I give myself the freedom to feel the grief, recognize it, and walk away from it.

Let me mention one other important thing here. Being present doesn't mean you can't learn from the past or plan for the future as Spencer Johnson wrote about. You can be in the present while being aware you are thinking back on something that has meaning to help where you are now. The same goes for the future. You can have a vision or plan for the future, while keeping your focus in the now. This is exactly what Buick was doing when he mentally prepared to fly.

He was in the present, learning from his experience of the past to visualize his future flight.

"Going back to find the beginning of an ending that now will rest. Walk away peaceful. Walk away free. Take

with you only those pieces the heart wants to see."

– Lyrics from Window Angel, written by Renée St. Cyr

Another great book about staying in the present is *How to Lose Your Mind in No Time*, by Hanaan Rosenthal. It's the type of book you can pick up over and over again and depending where you're at in life, it gives new meaning. Hanaan teaches to resist nothing, to let go, imagine, allow and then let go some more. He is an amazing tour guide on an enlightened journey of self-understanding.

So, how is this relevant to what you want to accomplish? Staying in the present moment keeps you focused. When you are working toward your goal, you want all your attention to be with the task at hand and you want it to stay there as much as possible. Don't beat yourself up if you start to wander. The more you're aware of staying in the moment, the better you'll get at it.

6 ATTITUDE IS EVERYTHING

"Give me a lever long enough and a place to stand, and I can move the Earth."
– Archimedes

YEARS ago, my dad was digging holes in the backyard to prepare for the installation of a fence. My older brother was helping him. They were laboring for some time, and suddenly their shovels hit something hard. They had struck a huge boulder. My brother immediately said there was no way just the two of them could get that boulder out of the ground. He went on and on about why it couldn't be done.

In the meantime, my father continued to think about the situation. He left for a few moments and returned with a large crowbar. My dad then asked my brother to get the garden hose and place it in the hole and turn the water on. The water started to loosen up the soil. Then they used the crowbar for leverage to eventually jimmy the boulder out of the ground.

When they were finished, my father calmly turned to my brother and said, "Take the "T" off of can't." My brother and I often use that phrase with our own kids today. Let's look at the following two scenarios:

Scenario One

A woman and her daughter are walking together on a sandy beach. The fluffy, white clouds suddenly give way to darker, more ominous skies.

The wind lashes at them, and they're caught in a torrential downpour.

The mother exclaims with dismay, "My God! Look at this weather! We are completely soaked!" The daughter responds with anger, "This is unbelievable!" The raindrops chill them to the bone and they feel like helpless children. The daughter shouts as she balls her fists to the sky and spins round and round, "Well, aren't we having a hell of a time!"

Scenario Two

A woman and her daughter are walking together on a sandy beach. The fluffy, white clouds suddenly give way to darker, more ominous skies. The wind lashes at them, and they're caught in a torrential downpour.

The mother exclaims with surprise, "My God! Look at this weather! We are completely soaked!" The daughter laughs, "This is unbelievable!" The mother laughs, too, and suddenly they feel like carefree children. The daughter shouts, as she stretches her arms to the sky and spins round and round, "Well, aren't we having a hell of a time!"

A similar situation happened a few weeks back with my mom and me. We chose scenario two. We couldn't control the weather, but we could control how we chose to acclimate ourselves to the situation.

You will be more successful if you are able to put yourself into the right frame of mind to proceed with the journey to your goal. As much as I hate to make assumptions, I'll assume you're still trying to get in the right frame of mind because you've chosen to read this book. Kudos to you! As you move forward and start to see your progress, this desire will keep you pumped to keep going. There's nothing more motivational than taking actionable steps and watching your accomplishments begin to unfold.

Yes, there will be setbacks. Or there will be days where you're just not into pursuing your dreams. That's ok. Sometimes you'll take two steps forward and one step back. But an amazing gift you have is the freedom of choice: you always have the option to choose to get back on track. Give yourself a break. When you fall, pick yourself up, dust yourself off and get moving again. Tell yourself to get out of your own way.

"So often times it happens that we live our lives in chains and we never even know we have the key."
– Already Gone, Eagles

7 WHAT'S HOLDING YOU BACK?

LET'S say it's always been a dream of yours to write a book and now you are finally ready to set a goal to achieve that dream. There's an excitement at first. As time goes on however, depending on how reachable your dream may be, perhaps you start to wane a bit on all that enthusiasm. Perhaps even a little bit of fear is starting to creep in. Perhaps you start to think you're not quite worthy of that dream. Maybe you hit a roadblock because you have to learn or do something that takes you out of your comfort zone. And there go the brakes! So what just happened? Well, there are at least a few things going on.

Your Brain Hates Change

Neuroscience research has recently shown through MRI scans that the brain often struggles with change, so any type of goal, especially one that introduces behavioral change, is a tall order. The brain is conditioned to seek pleasure and avoid pain. The limbic system in the brain controls emotions. A perceived threat, such as change, can have a strong impact on the limbic system. So, initially when you're faced with even a small notion such as facing the unknown on a task that arises, your brain goes on alert and you put up resistance to creativity, new thinking and judgment. You freeze up. It's the mountain out of the molehill effect. I know there are times I've visited that mountain.

When I started my website, The Passion to Pursue, I was eager and excited! I could see the end game in my head, visualizing what the website would look like. I figured out my tasks and off I went! Before long, I realized that yes, I could get a website up and running fairly quickly, but it wasn't going to be all that easy if I wanted to customize it.

I found myself having to learn how to code. I admit I didn't see that one coming! And how did I react? I got frustrated and I froze up. Here was a time consuming and challenging task not taken into consideration. So I figured I had a few options. I could bug my partner from one of my other business ventures, who's a coding guru (ok, I admit asking a question of her here and there!), hire someone, or learn it myself. I made the decision to learn how to code and it definitely took me out of my comfort zone, but something really cool happened along the way. I had an all out brawl with my limbic brain and won! The feeling of success and accomplishment of that task reminded me that it's not all about the end game; it's also about the journey. What this also did was to give me more confidence for when I have to face the next challenge that comes along.

I do have to say here however, try not to get too consumed in tasks that take you away from your dream. Being productive and continuing to move ahead in a timely fashion with your tasks is the best way to go. Learning to code may not have been the best path to choose if I were under a tight deadline to launch my website. For me, I thought through the pros & cons and knew deep down it was something I really did want to learn more about for future endeavors.

Drawback Of Only Focusing On The End Game

Dreams are often sabotaged long before they come into existence. Often people see reaching a goal as all or nothing; 99% just isn't enough. I say hogwash to that.

As I was learning to code, I was celebrating a win. As I was picking out the fonts to use on my site, the color schemes, and the pictures to use—they were all a wonderful cause for celebration. Yes, accomplishing your dream is an amazing feeling, but it would be terrible to miss out on all that's accomplished along the way.

No Control Over Outcomes

Sometimes, no matter how much effort you put into something, the truth of the matter is that you will never be able to have full control of its outcome. As the saying goes, sh@t happens. No matter how much you try to plan, you can't take all the variables into account. Sure, you can do a fine job of getting as much as you can planned and organized, but you still need to be willing to accept that the outcome may not be exactly what you wanted. Whether or not you've reached your dream, it's important to remember how much you've grown from your experiences. Each time you face a new challenge you become stronger to face the next unknown.

"Happiness in life is about stepping into necessary uncertainty and not needing to know the outcome— because if we are honest, we rarely, if ever, know. All of life is a giant leap of faith. And what holds us back is the obsessive and debilitating need for certainty of outcome ahead of time. But that is not how life works. Life requires faith, boldness and courage to step into the unknown with the knowing that my heart and intuition

are always guiding me and know the way. As I step out of the way, a way will be made."

– Mastin Kipp

Everyone Is Afraid Of Facing The Unknown

I don't care who you are or what it is you're trying to accomplish. We're all in this together. Anyone who has achieved something in life has had to overcome fear in one capacity or another.

I recently read, *Lean In: Women, Work, and the Will to Lead,* written by Sheryl Sandberg, who is the current chief operating officer at Facebook. There is a section where she boldly admits to being afraid about learning new skills. Here's an excerpt from the book you might find interesting.

"If I'm afraid to do something, it is usually because I am not good at it or perhaps am too scared even to try. After working at Google for more than

four years, managing well over half of the company's revenues, I was embarrassed to admit that I had never negotiated a business deal. Not one. So I gathered my courage and came clean to my boss, Omid Kordestani, then head of sales and business development. Omid was willing to give me a chance to run a small deal team. In the very first deal I attempted, I almost botched the whole thing by making an offer to our potential partner before fully understanding their business. Fortunately, my team included a talented negotiator, Shailesh Rao, who stepped in to teach me the obvious: letting the other side make the first offer is often crucial to achieving favorable terms."

Not only admitting to a fear, but also actually taking the steps to overcome it is the name of the game. Sure, Sheryl Sandberg made mistakes, but the important thing is that she learned from them and I have no doubt she's managed to negotiate more than a few successful business deals since then.

It's Ok To Mess Up

As I look back on my corporate years, I know one of the biggest reasons I was able to become successful and continue to make my way up the ranks was due to the type of boss I had. We had lunch a few weeks back and I thanked him. I thanked him for giving me the freedom to take chances. Yes, sometimes I didn't measure up to my own expectations, but I showed up and gave my best. If things didn't go according to plan, I took ownership of what happened, learned from it and came out ahead for myself, my boss and the company the next time around.

Now, there may be some of you out there that are saying, "Yeah, that's great Renée, but unfortunately, I don't happen to work in a place with a safe environment where I'm able to make a mistake and learn from it." First, proceed with caution. Take on smaller tasks that won't cause significant damage in the long run. Hopefully, little by little your boss and the company will see cutting some slack to take some calculated chances could go a long way for productivity. And if they don't, perhaps you should consider working elsewhere!

So the next time you're faced with a challenge, be it at work, something for self-improvement or wanting to take the first steps in pursing a dream, face the fear, have some faith and take that leap!

And how do you stop yourself from being held back?

1. Be Aware! Look for the signs that your emotional, limbic brain is coming in for a landing. If you face a challenge and you start to freeze up, recognize it, catch yourself and tell yourself there's a workaround. Try to keep from climbing up the sheer face of the mountain in your mind (remember visualization?) Start on the scenic path.

2. Enjoy The Ride! Remember: it's not just about finally reaching that goal; it's also about all you learn along the way and feeling great about each achievement no matter how small.

3. Let It Go! I know this is a tough one for a lot of people, including me. Do all you can to get to where you want to be, but remember that you can't control everything and perhaps by letting go even just a bit, you may be surprised at how well things still turn out.

4. It's Ok To Make Mistakes! We all do it. You're not alone in this. It's important to show up, own it, learn from it, and move on.

"Hell, there are no rules here— we're just trying to accomplish something."

– Thomas A. Edison

8 IS THIS REALLY WHAT YOU NEED TO GET WHAT YOU WANT?

HERE it comes... the voice of reason. Ugh! I don't want to discourage you, but this is a very good time to really examine that dream of yours. When you think of reaching that goal, what emotions does it conjure up? When you envision yourself at the finish line, ask yourself this: could there perhaps be things in your life that already give you that same pleasure? What I'm trying to get at is whether or not that grass *is* always greener.

I've watched people strive after something, only to see them realize that after all their hard work, it really wasn't what they wanted in the first place, or at the very least their perception of the dream didn't match up to the reality of the dream.

People can get bored and feel hollow if they try to fill their lives up with the clutter of possessions that ultimately don't make them happy or help them to find peace.

I recently came across a commencement speech, *This Is Water*, given to the Kenyan College class of 2005, by David Foster Wallace. Mr. Wallace was an author and professor, who unfortunately died tragically in 2008.

There were many parts I found intriguing, but as I read the following words, all I could think about was this particular chapter of my book. He went on to say;

"If you worship money and things, if they are where you tap real meaning in life, then you will never

have enough, never feel you have enough. It's the truth. Worship your body and beauty and sexual allure and you will always feel ugly. And when time and age start showing, you will die a million deaths before they finally grieve you. On one level, we all know this stuff already. It's been codified as myths, proverbs, clichés, epigrams, parables; the skeleton of every great story. The whole trick is keeping the truth up front in daily consciousness."

"They're the kind of worship you just gradually slip into, day after day, getting more and more selective about what you see and how you measure value without ever being fully aware that that's what you're doing."

This is pretty deep stuff, yet also simplistic. I don't believe Mr. Wallace is saying you should avoid going after tangible things, which will bring meaning to your life. For example, if your goal is to own a sailboat, that boat may end up being something that brings joy to you, family members and friends for years to come. What you want to steer clear of is the constant need for a bigger and better boat. Eventually, you could just end up on autopilot and be missing out on the amazing ride of the here and now.

And maybe, just maybe, a handful of things in life will not be attainable. This chapter is in no way meant to bring you down from that high you feel whenever you think of pursuing your dream. If there are sacrifices to make, be sure they don't outweigh the good of the dream. If you're thinking of a career change, there's nothing keeping you from perhaps first volunteering in that field a few hours a week to see if it's really for you. And sometimes your dreams may work out in ways you'd least expect.

My Dreams Take A Turn

Years ago, I had a dream to teach elementary school. I already had a bachelor's degree in business, and I decided to go back to college in the evenings to earn my teaching certification. It was two years of hard work, topped off with six months of student teaching.

I was in the elementary classroom doing my teaching from 7:00 -11:00 a.m. I then had just under an hour to drive into Boston where I worked from noon to 9:00 p.m. I got home at 10:00 p.m., wrote lesson plans and graded papers until midnight and started all over again the next morning. I was doing it: I was pursuing my dream to teach, but a funny thing happened along the way.

I started to grow close to the people I worked with in Boston and the company I worked for. I was advancing in my career and found myself torn between my dream to teach and my growing interest in my corporate career. My heart and my gut were beginning to shift. I eventually landed a teaching position, gave my notice in Boston and believe it or not, I was back at my company by the end of the week!

I unknowingly entered my teaching position under very strained and awkward circumstances that took me all of two days to catch on to. I walked into a political hornet's nest. I made the difficult choice of informing the superintendent of schools of my intention to leave before the children grew attached. My previous company took me back with open arms, no questions asked. I admit I did feel a little bit silly. They had just given me a going away party! But I knew I was ok when a bouquet of flowers was delivered to me with a note from the CFO that said, "What took you so long to come back?" And Human Resources chalked it up to me losing my key and having another assigned. At the time, that was the amazing place with the amazing people I couldn't give up.

So what happened to my dream in that situation? I listened to my heart, to my gut and I trusted my instincts. Was the teaching certification a waste of time? No, absolutely not. If I could get through to a class of 28 fourth graders for a half year, I could talk in front of anyone! It seriously helped me during times that I spoke in public or needed to give training sessions to a large group of people. And I was able to volunteer my Saturday mornings to help out inner-city kids on a mentoring/academic basis. So you see, I still did achieve my dream of teaching. I still had time with kids, and I also trained adults in a corporate setting. My dream came in a way I wouldn't have expected!

As you figure out your dreams, be sure to stay open, flexible and go with the flow. The following Aesop's Fable demonstrates how flexibility gives us strength.

The Oak And The Reeds

A mighty oak tree was uprooted by a gale and fell across a stream into some reeds. "How have you reeds, so frail, survived, when I, so strong, have been felled?" asked the oak tree. "You were stubborn and wouldn't bend," replied the reeds, "Whereas we yield and allow the gale to pass harmlessly by."

So, just take that extra time to think through what you really want. Then, once you've decided, don't let anything or anyone stop you and remember your goals may end up being accomplished in ways you could have never predicted.

9 DEFINE WHAT IT IS

THESE days, it seems everywhere you turn you read or hear about people trying to find a sense of purpose, things you do for yourself or others that gives life meaning. You may already know what you'd like to pursue (or for that matter, even just things you feel you need to get done), but if not, I would like to suggest that you look at this from another angle. Try not to get hung up on realizing your sense of purpose; rather let it come to you. For a time you may consider putting yourself through a little test of self-discovery.

Note: Remember I mentioned at the beginning of the book that where you see the symbol (+), it's an indicator to take some type of action? Well, here you go!

(+) Over the next few days, try to become more aware of the situations that bring you joy or contentment. Jot down exactly what it was you were doing that brought those feelings about. Then do the same thing with situations that give you feelings of unhappiness or discomfort. What you'll start to see is a pattern that may very well help you find out what gives you a sense of purpose.

Toward the end of this book is a resource area. There you will find a chart that you can use for recording your information.

Call It A Hunch

Earlier when I mentioned heading back to my firm after leaving my teaching position, I said that I listened to my heart, to my gut and I trusted my instincts. For me, it's usually either a good or a bad feeling I get when weighing out options. I'll think about something, open myself up to it and most times I go along with what my heart is trying to tell me. The few times that I don't listen up are usually due to some type of fear that I need to first recognize, admit to and then to have the guts (pun intended) to get over it and move on.

There is some debate on the origins of intuition. Some may say it's from an inner source or a higher power. There is also a more scientific explanation. Dr. Helen Fisher states:

"While intuition may seem to arise from some mysterious inner source, it's actually a form of unconscious

reasoning—one that's rooted in the way our brains collect and store information.

As you accumulate knowledge— whether it's about what books your spouse likes or how to play chess— you begin to recognize patterns. Your brain unconsciously organizes these patterns into blocks of information—a process the late social scientist Herbert Simon, PhD, called chunking. Over time your brain chunks and links more and more patterns, then stores these clusters of knowledge in your long-term memory. When you see a tiny detail of a familiar design, you instantly recognize the larger composition—and that's what we regard as a flash of intuition."

– Fisher, Helen, PhD. "When to Listen to Your Gut...and When Not To." O, The Oprah Magazine. July 2010: Print.

And most interesting as of late is how the military is weighing in on the concept of intuition. On February 29, 2012, the Office of Naval Research launched a special notice for the Basic Research Challenge of exploring the Enhancing Intuitive Decision Making Process Through Implicit Learning [Solicitation Number: 12-SN-0007, Agency: Department of the Navy, Office: Office of Naval Research, Location: ONR].

The Navy set aside $3.85 million to be used over a four-year period for researchers who want to explore how members of the military can improve on their intuitive ability or rather their sixth sense. This has come up largely due to the testimony of soldiers, which have reported feelings of danger prior to encountering an attack. The scientists managing the program have gone so far as to describe what the soldiers are feeling as their "Spidey sense" tingling, comparing it to the intuitiveness of the Marvel comic book character, Spiderman.

No matter the origin, listening to your intuition may help to hold the key that you are on the right track for whatever it is you're looking to set out to accomplish. As you move forward, take the time to check in with yourself on occasion to make sure what's stirring around in your gut still feels right. If not, continue to change course until it starts to feel right again.

"We can't direct the wind, but we can adjust the sails."
– Thomas S. Monson

10 IT'S TIME TO GO & GET IT!

NOW, it's time to create your Go & Get It Method List, which will contain the wants and needs that you would like to pursue. This is your time to discover and brainstorm. There are no wrong answers here.

The following *eight steps* will guide you through the process.

1. Make Time For Yourself To Get The Work Done—Toss The Guilt

(+) Open your calendar and schedule what I call Me Time. Carve out some time where you know you don't have to do anything for anyone but yourself. I know putting yourself first might take some getting used to, but it's mandatory if you want to see your dreams start to unfold. I know there will always be those who need something of you, but during Me Time, try really hard to put yourself ahead of the pack. This may sound selfish, but in the long run, it really isn't.

I'm sure for those who fly, a few of you out there watch attentively as the flight attendants' offer their safety demonstration before takeoff. They say if the oxygen masks fall from the ceiling compartments for any reason, you are to place the mask on your face first, and then assist others around you. As a mother, my first instinct would be to get the mask on my sons. After some thought however, it does make perfect sense to go first. You can't help your kids put on their masks if you have stopped breathing.

To realistically keep things moving along during and after your list is complete, you should try to block out at least two hours of time at least three times a week, if not more. This timetable isn't set in stone, however you seriously need to give yourself the time to work through the Go & Get It! Method process, which we'll soon discuss. This should be treated as a top priority in your life, with the same importance as getting your kids to basketball practice, a doctor's appointment, or going to meetings at work.

2. Find A Place Of Comfort

Where you spend your Me Time is an important consideration. Start to think of somewhere that you'll feel comfortable and have room to spread out. Maybe it's a blanket on the beach or perhaps even a table for one at a favorite restaurant. Just make sure you spend this time alone!

3. Purchase Your Supplies

(+) For now, your supplies will consist of pencils & stickies (Post-it notes). I LOVE stickies. Let me repeat that. I LOVE stickies! A few years back I was taking classes at Boston University for Project Management. The best thing that came out of those classes was the versatile use of stickies when it comes to organizing your thoughts. You'll see how as you move ahead, but for now, bookmark this page and let's say adieu, au revoir, sa-yo-na-ra, see you later alligator, until we meet again during that Me Time you carved out for yourself. Then you can begin right back...

Here! Welcome to your place of comfort. I hope you remembered your pencil & stickies. Let's begin to explore and define your dreams and goals.

4. Get Into The Right Frame Of Mind

First things are first. You've got to slowwww down your thoughts. Like I've already talked about, Nellie who lives inside all our heads, loves to distract us from what's important.

(+) So, start by taking some deep breaths in and out of your nose. They should be really deep breaths, so when you breathe in, your belly is sticking way out there and when you breathe out your stomach deflates like a balloon. Close your eyes if you like. You'll know where you should be when your heartbeat has slowed down and you begin to feel relaxed. Now might also be a great time for you to have a glass of wine or herbal tea!

5. Think What You Want

(+) Let all your focus be in the present moment and begin to think about all the things you WANT to do. These would be considered nice to haves. There are no wrong answers. Just take your time and begin to picture them.

(+) As soon as your ideas start coming into focus, grab your supplies. Start writing down each individual idea or item on a single sticky note and stick it onto a flat surface, *i.e.,* a wall, a desk, a beach blanket, your car dashboard (in a parked car of course!). There doesn't have to be any order. You can stick them on a surface randomly for now. Just keep writing. Keep it simple. They should be short phrases. For example, learn to sail, go back to school, play the piano.

(+) When you've exhausted your thoughts on what you've always wanted to do, take all your stickies, put them in a pile and set them aside. Feel good about this! It is a huge accomplishment!

6. Think What You Need

(+) Next, center yourself again with some really deep breaths. This time start to think about all the things you NEED to get done. I mean tasks that go beyond the day-to-day, routine stuff. These should be tasks that need some forethought and planning such as making arrangements for your parents' 50th wedding anniversary, organizing volunteers for community events. Now you know what to do: start writing on those stickies! Again, when finished, gather them all up and set aside. This process may take more than one sitting and that's totally fine.

7. Arrange Stickies In Order You Want To Proceed

When you think you've exhausted all your ideas, you can then move on to organizing your stickies. You've got to figure out what you'd like or what you have to do first, second, third, and so on.

(+) Go through the first stack of your "wants" stickies and spread them out again. Begin organizing your goals in the order of importance. Once you're finished, do the same with the other stack of "needs" and then combine the stacks together.

How you order both stacks is up to you, however, mixing and matching the wants versus the needs will help give a sense of balance in your life. I'd suggest you begin with the absolutes or those that are more time sensitive and then sprinkle in the rest.

8. Write Out Your Go & Get It! Method List

(+) Take each sticky and type or write up your wants/needs list in the order you think you would like to proceed. Earlier in the process, you used short phrases on each sticky. You can keep it as such. Just be sure to write enough to capture the essence of your goal. This is your Go & Get

It! Method List. It can be as long as you like or as short as you like. Nothing is set in stone. This is a live document, which means the order can change due to life circumstances and interests. Just having it will always keep you on track for what you could pursue should you have the need or desire to do so.

Myth Of Multitasking

You may find at times that you would like to take on more than one goal at a time. This is certainly doable, however, it will take more planning on your part. For example, as I write this book, another ongoing goal is to continue to enhance and maintain my website, The Passion to Pursue. As long as a good, solid plan is in place for both, I can move back and forth between the two. This doesn't mean multitasking, which I see as a fallacy. We humans were not wired to perform more than one task at a time. I watched people at work try this over and over again, thinking they were getting more accomplished. But in fact, the opposite was true. Their attention was constantly being shifted from one thing to the next, and they continued to waste time trying to pick up the pieces of where they last left off. You can only do one thing at a time. But yes, you can work toward multiple goals as long as you stay focused on the task at hand and you have a smooth way to transition to whatever it is you need or want to do next. This will also require some time management skills, which I will soon discuss.

As time goes by, perhaps you will have tackled only one goal, but gave it your all. Or maybe you've flown through each and every goal. This is your story and no one else's, so whatever you've achieved is just perfect.

Paul McCartney was once asked if he had any regrets that some early songs he wrote with John Lennon were never recorded. I'm paraphrasing here but he said something like, "If a song isn't remembered, it isn't meant to be." For every *Let It Be* (I'm glad they remembered that one), they had thousands of other ideas that didn't make it. And that's ok, just like not getting to all your goals is ok. I guarantee, however, that you'll be satisfied when you just let it be and you can be proud of every step you take toward something wonderful.

PART II

FROM this point on, you will be working toward creating your Go & Get It! Method Plan. This plan is a roadmap that will outline the defined process for the first item on your Go & Get It! Method List and it will pave the way for you to reach your goal or intention. In the coming chapters, there are *fourteen steps* that will guide you through the process.

11 MISSION STATEMENT

THE first item for your Go & Get It! Method Plan will be the creation of a mission statement. This is a summary of the aims and values of a company, organization or an individual person. It essentially helps give credence to a goal. There's nothing better than seeing a paragraph or even just a few sentences right out there to keep you on track with your dream. It should be very simple and to the point. It can be as long or as short as you like, however, I would advise trying to keep it somewhat brief so you can read it quickly to reinforce the work you're doing to reach your goal. It should align with your goal. For my album, my mission statement was simply worded:

"I want to release the music I hear inside me and share it with others."

When Steve Jobs was taking a leave of absence from Apple, Tim Cook, then COO of Apple, made a statement that could be taken as a mission statement. Cook was explaining what Apple stands for whether or not Steve Jobs still continued to be a part of the company. As you'll see below, Tim Cook's statement is a bit longer than a sentence, however, the idea is well thought out and easy to grasp.

"We believe that we're on the face of the earth to make great products and that's not changing. We're constantly focusing on innovating. We believe in the simple, not the complex.

We believe we need to own and control the primary technologies behind the products that we make and participate only in markets where we can make a significant contribution.

We believe in saying no to thousands of projects so that we can focus on the few that are meaningful to us.

We believe in deep collaboration and cross-pollination in order to innovate in a way others cannot.

We don't settle for anything other than excellence in any group in the company, and we have the self-honesty to admit when we're wrong and the courage to change."

Note: Again, take heed to Tim Cook's words above, "We believe in saying no to thousands of projects so that we can focus on the few that are meaningful to us." This is an excellent example to follow for you as well.

Here's another example of a shorter mission statement. I think this one from Walmart is great!

"To give ordinary folk the chance to buy the same thing as rich people."

1. Start On Your First Item

(+) Take the time to really reflect on the first item of your Go & Get It! Method List. This is your first, most important goal.

2. Create A Mission Statement

(+) Write out a statement that reflects that goal and ultimately this will become your mission statement. Be sure to display it in an area where you will be able to look at it frequently. By referring to this mission statement, your heart and gut will continue to help you stay the course. A great time to refer to your mission is when you hit those milestones, which I will talk about soon.

12 ACTION ITEMS

WELCOME back to our old, sticky pals! This time around, you'll start fresh and be using them to guide your actions and eventually itemize what you have to do in an organized flow.

You now have the first item—your goal—from your Go & Get It! Method List. And hopefully you've put some thought into a mission statement and it's being boldly displayed somewhere you can refer back to it frequently.

3. Write Each Action Item On A Sticky

(+) Now it's time to write out individual action items on sticky notes, which takes you closer to achieving that goal on your list. Action items are some type of documented task that needs to take place. At this point, the notes should not be in any order. Don't spend even a second on trying to figure out any type of structure; it should all be freethinking.

Before you begin, it's important to notice that these items are ACTION items. Can you see the difference between the two statements below?

- Inventory needed of all rough, recorded songs
- Take inventory of all rough, recorded songs

The first sentence is just a statement. The second is where you are telling yourself to take action.

"Commitment leads to action. Action brings your dream closer."
– Marcia Wieder

Here's an example of a few stickies from when I was creating my first album. There were hundreds of overwhelming items I had to take care of. So I began with...

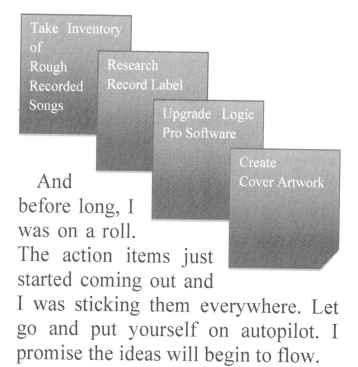

And before long, I was on a roll. The action items just started coming out and I was sticking them everywhere. Let go and put yourself on autopilot. I promise the ideas will begin to flow.

You may not have all the answers and that's ok. Go back and take a look at my second sticky again. It said, research record label. Before I started out, I knew I wanted my album to be independently distributed, but I had no idea where to begin, so I researched it. I began to learn all the ins and outs of starting my own record label. At that stage in the process, it was just enough for me to know I needed to look into it. As time went on however, I knew I needed to learn as much as I could. There are also times where using the expertise of someone else may be more time effective. Make sure your self-education doesn't detract too much from your ultimate goal and schedule. By outsourcing you can gain from the knowledge and expertise of others.

Something To Bear In Mind—Do You Really Need This Task?

From here on in, you'll be referring to your action items as tasks. You established actions that are now turning into tasks that need to get done. The idea is to always consider,

"Do you really need this task(s) to get to the next task?" More times than not, you will. Again, this is where those amazing sticky notes come in handy.

If a task isn't really needed, just crumple it up and aim for the recycling bin. Right now, a whole lot of time should be spent brainstorming and switching up those sticky notes. Once it's all laid out, it's easier to see if all the tasks are needed and if they're in the right order. *The more you do at this point in the process, the less you have to worry about what comes next later on.* This is your personalized roadmap. Once it's in place, be sure not to spend a minute more than you have to on organizing and updating—spend your time on the tasks themselves—working toward your dream.

13 TIME TO ORGANIZE

YOU should now have a collection of colorful stickies. Can you believe how very much you've accomplished already and how you are that much closer to achieving your goal?

4. Organize Tasks Within Each Bucket Sequentially

Next, you'll take all those tasks and start to see where they may fall into similar categories, or what you'll refer to as buckets.

with The Passion to Pursue, I had the following notes: create a website, a Twitter account, create a Facebook page and so on. These all started flowing into what I thought should be a marketing bucket. Some might not fit that well into any group. These may end up being standalone items, and that's Ok.

(+) Take all the like-minded stickies and start organizing them into

buckets. As you do so, now you should also start to consider the logical ordering of each action item. This is where the ease of mixing and matching really comes in handy with the stickies. You can switch them up as much as you need until everything looks like it might be in the right order within the right bucket. Be sure to keep dependencies in mind. A dependency is some type of action you have to take before you can go on to the next action item.

For example, before I started any new vocal recordings, I had to upgrade my Logic Pro software. Before I upgraded my software, I had to purchase the upgrade. Before I started the upgrade, I had to back up my system, etc.

Here are some of the actions items I categorized in an appropriate order into one bucket:

- Review application requirements

- Backup system

- Purchase Logic Pro upgrade

- Install upgrade

- Review release notes

- Compare to older recordings

5. Name That Bucket

(+) You have your buckets and it's time to figure out a name for each if you haven't done so already. As explained earlier, my Twitter account, Facebook and website started to look like they would fit into a marketing bucket, so that is what the name became.

6. Organize Your Buckets Sequentially

(+) You're ready to take your buckets (that are now named and contain all your tasks in an order that makes sense to you) and organize them in a logical sequence. Ask yourself, "How should I logically order my buckets?" In Chapter 17, I'll be discussing some different options; you'll have to be able to visually lay out all the information you're now in the process of organizing.

For organizing purposes, let's take the holiday, Thanksgiving for an example. It's your turn to host this year and you want things to run as smoothly as they can. I won't go into an entire scenario here, but just enough to help further explain your buckets and their ordering.

Let's say you've already spent time brainstorming, you've come up with tasks that need to get done and they've fallen under the following buckets: cleaning, grocery shopping, cooking, decorations, organizing dinnerware, etc. When you look at these buckets, you can start to identify what needs to get done first, second and so on. So, maybe a logical order for your buckets at this point would be:

- Cleaning
- Decorations
- Grocery shopping
- Organizing dinnerware
- Cooking

And within these buckets, you would have all the sequential tasks associated with each bucket.

So when you're done, you should have a few stacks of stickies. The top sticky for each stack should have the bucket name on it. You can set these stacks aside for now and you'll get back to them in Chapter 18.

14 OH, I GET BY WITH A LITTLE HELP FROM MY FRIENDS

7. Find Your Resources

So far, this book has focused on a one-person show and I know you're very good at that. At times, however, you may need to reach out to others for help. Perhaps there are items on that task list that you might not be able to handle on your own. There are a number of ways to seek out help.

Perhaps you have an easier time giving then receiving. What you need to remember is how good it feels to be on the giving end of things so when you're receiving, you'll know that people want to help just as much as you do, and it makes them feel good to do so. Thankfully, the older I get, the more I'm willing to gratefully receive from others. What is important is making sure you're able to show your appreciation.

There may be times when you'd feel more comfortable giving something back in return. Even if it's just a small token or gesture.

For example, I asked a very talented, long time friend of mine to help out with the cover of my album. We had fun with the process, and in the end he wanted nothing for it. I gave him credit on the album and website, and then I surprised him with a heart felt thank-you note and told him to enjoy an evening out with his lovely wife and that I would pick up the tab. Perhaps you have a skill or talent you can barter with. I have done this in the past as well and it has turned out equally beneficial.

When you need help and your inner circle may not have the expertise you're looking for, you may have to spend some money to find the right resource, but you don't necessarily have to break the bank.

There is one website which I would like to recommend where I've had very good results. The company is called Fiverr (fiverr.com).

It's basically a marketplace for professional and creative services if that might be something you're in need of. The amazing thing is that the initial cost of what they call a "gig," is $5.00.

You essentially post a request, get offers from a broad array of talented people living globally, place an order and then you're notified when the work is complete. If you end up with a lot of changes on a particular project, you may start getting charged incrementally on the turnarounds. The more efficient and articulate you are with your instructions, the less it will cost you.

For example, I did most of the work for the cover of this book. I knew the artwork I wanted to use and the layout, but I wasn't sure on the best use of color on the background and text. I used clear instructions on what I was looking for and the cover was complete in one turnaround! I did end up gladly paying the designer another $10.00 for a 3D image of the book to use on my website and I then topped it off with a generous tip because I was so happy with the work. I will say however, buyers beware! Make sure to check the Buyers Reviews. I am happy to report that I've only had one instance where a deliverable was not what I had asked for and after some negotiation, I was able to get a refund and move on. Take the time to do a little vetting and you should be good to go.

Whichever way you end up finding help, you'll eventually refer to these folks in your Go & Get It! Method Plan as *resources*.

8. Recognize And Appreciate Your Milestones

I love milestones! Not as much as stickies, but they're a close second. Milestones are places you reach after all your tasks are complete from a particular bucket. And you'll love to watch progress as it's being made! It's a great feeling to reach a milestone and a wonderful time to celebrate. The celebration can be something simple that has meaning to you. When you reach a milestone, go out dancing, go buy yourself an ice cream, get a massage or get to that movie you've been dying to see. Above all else, be proud of what you've accomplished!

One of the buckets for my album project was titled: Organization of Rough Song Material. Within this bucket I had the following tasks: clean all song files on MacBook Pro, take inventory of all songs, select focus group of song choices, create questionnaire for song choices, and set up listening time of samples. My next bucket was called Protection. Again, I had a list of tasks I needed to complete, such as copyright and song licensing.

When I completed the last task in my first bucket, which was set up listening time of samples, this is where I reached a milestone. I was between the end of a segment of tasks and the beginning of new ones.

(+) As I talked about earlier, reaching milestones is a good time throughout the project to do a check in. Take a long, hard look at your mission statement. Are you still on track? What are your heart and your gut telling you? If you're still not on course, ask yourself why and adjust accordingly.

16 TIMING IS EVERYTHING

9. Think About A Timeline

FOR a plan to succeed, time management has to play a role. This is basically being consciously aware of the amount of time it takes to do a specific task. Others may think differently, but I can't see the sense of letting something go on and on without some type of timeframe. This does not mean you have to assign time for tasks right down to the minute. This would become cumbersome and would more than likely take the fun out of what you're setting out to do.

Some tasks may take a few minutes, others a few hours and some perhaps days. It will be up to you to project an appropriate timeframe for each task. In the next chapter, I will talk about setting up a designated area in your plan where you'll be able to fill in deadlines.

Deadlines may not exactly make you feel warm and fuzzy, but you just can't do without them. Being held accountable is key for anything to get off the ground. Remember to factor in those couple of hours you've already set aside each week on your calendar. Don't bite off more than you can chew. You don't want to set yourself up for disappointment. Be firm, yet realistic with yourself. You'll also have to factor in those resources—any others who may be helping you out. Communication is key: don't make assumptions about their time. Once you have a good idea on timing for yourself, go to them and ask what is reasonable.

Just having a plan in and of itself will be a tremendous help to keep you on track with your time. Limiting your distractions will also help a great deal. You are busy and pulled in a million different directions, but try hard to hold on to your Me Time, and then fit in more time whenever you get the chance.

Taking breaks is also extremely helpful. Whether you're doing something of a physical nature, like building that shed you always wanted, or you're sitting down to write a novel, taking breaks are key. Back in my corporate days, I tried to get away from my desk and walk for 30 minutes a day. I would just leave it all behind. I would walk for 15 minutes, turn around and walk back. It had to be one of the most effective things I did all day to increase my own productivity. I always came back alert, refreshed, and ready to dig into the next task at hand. Since I usually sat for many hours each day, 30 minutes was adequate time to clear my head. If you're working with 2-hour intervals for your Me Time, give yourself a short breather after the first hour. Stand up in place and stretch or go grab yourself a cup of tea.

I have one last important piece of advice on the subject. Whenever possible, set time aside to work on your goal when you often feel most productive. I'm sure you have some idea as to whether you're a morning or evening person.

I am very much a morning person. I'm out of bed early, generally refreshed and ready to start the day. This is when I feel most productive. By evening however, I am just ready to relax and hit the hay relatively early. Listen to your internal clock and plan accordingly whenever you're able.

17 WHERE DO YOU LAY IT ALL OUT?

10. Decide Where To Lay Out Your Information

THERE are a number of places and a number of ways you can lay out your Go & Get It! Method Plan. You don't have to use a fancy software application. In fact, paper and a pencil or a whiteboard will do the trick. But if you decide to look at applications, there are a whole lot to choose from.

You want something that is going to help you organize tasks, while staying on a reasonable timeline. What you don't want is an application that's going to slow things down. It's counterproductive to spend all your time managing a process tool rather than actually doing the tasks that need to be done to get you closer to the finish line.

In this chapter I'll provide some options for you to explore. Please keep in mind that everyone works a bit differently. Some people like to see lists; others like visuals. I like both. One visual, a Gantt Chart, developed by Henry Gantt, is great when working with the progress of tasks. This bar-style chart is commonly used by project managers to illustrate the project's schedule.

Tom's Planner

After some lengthy research, I was able to narrow down my search to an application called Tom's Planner. It's described as a web-based planning

application.
http://www.tomsplanner.com/.
I was looking for an application with little or no learning curve. And with Tom's Planner, I was up and running within 20 minutes! A great feature they offer is existing templates in areas such as wedding planning, holiday planning, or managing rentals. Your goal may not necessarily fit in any of their categories, but it's a good resource to browse through, to show how you may want to set up your project.

It's available in the following web browsers: Internet Explorer 8 or higher and recent versions of Firefox, Chrome and Safari on Mac, PC, Linux, Chrome OS and/or iOS (iPad & iPhone).

As for operating systems, it works with Windows (PC), OS X (Mac), Linux (Ubuntu), Chrome OS (Google) and iOS (iPad and iPhone) and Android version 4 and up. For one user and one plan (they call it a schedule), it's free. If you want more than that, it will cost you, but it's reasonably priced with a number of options to choose from.

GanttProject

GanttProject, (ganttproject.biz) is a tool for project scheduling and management. Its interface isn't as glamorous as Tom's Planner, but it certainly does the trick.

It runs on Windows, Linux and MacOSX. Its code is open source and best of all it's free! Another great feature is its print capabilities. You have many formats to choose from. I created a PDF, which automatically included a cover sheet, the Gantt Chart, and a tasks list. There's a description area on the cover sheet that fits the bill for your mission statement.

Figure 1, gives an example of how the information can be laid out and viewed. Column 1 shows bucket labels, listing tasks below. Columns 2 and 3, list the start and end dates. Column 4 identifies any resources and column 5 lists the progress. A visual timeframe is shown on the right-hand side.

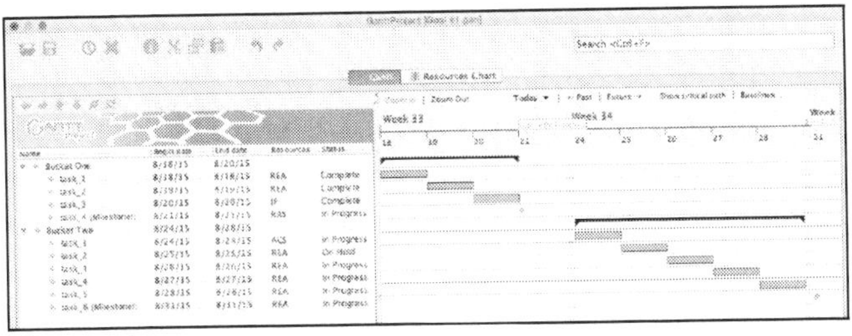

Figure 1

Excel Or Numbers Spreadsheet

If you use Excel, which is part of the Microsoft Office suite, Numbers within Apple's iCloud, or possibly open source software, LibreOffice, then just creating a spreadsheet might be enough for you. Similar to *Figure 1*, tasks could be itemized along the left-hand column and your rows on top could be listed with a start date, an end date, resources if any other than yourself, and the status. As each task is completed, you could highlight the row with a designated completion color. The more colorful your spreadsheet, the more you are getting accomplished!

Paper & Pencil

If you want to use the tried and true method of paper & pencil, go for it! If you decide to try something different, then take this time, (but not too much of it!) to explore other options on your own. Remember, you don't want to get bogged down on the tools. The focus should be on the tasks. Once you do choose and bring yourself up-to-speed, you'll be moving along in no time!

18 TIME TO START WRITING UP YOUR PLAN

THE pieces of the puzzle are now ready to fit into place.

1. A mission statement
2. Buckets with sequential tasks
3. Resources
4. Thoughts on a timeline

By now you have decided where your information is going to be laid out. Perhaps it will be in Tom's Planner, GanttProject, a spreadsheet, paper & pencil, a whiteboard or whatever you've come up with on your own.

11. Fill In Your Go & Get It! Method Plan

(+) It's time to say so long to your stickies. You need to get the action items off the stickies and start listing them as sequential tasks.

- Begin where you decided to lay out your information, i.e., Tom's Planner, GanttProject.

- Label your first bucket.

- Take each sticky associated with that bucket and transpose each task sequentially.

- Crumple up sticky and aim for the recycling bin. Score!

- Repeat for each bucket and associated tasks.

- Assign a start date for each task.

- Assign an end date for each task. And remember to be firm, but realistic on the dates. You can always go back and readjust them if need be.

- Fill in your resources (after you've chatted it up big time on how it will conveniently fit into their schedules).

- Status—at this point the status remains blank. As time goes on you can label the stage the tasks are in. For example, in progress, on-hold, complete, etc. Set up a fixed, reoccurring time to quickly update your plan to ensure you modify and stay on plan.

12. Start In On Your Tasks

Congratulations! You've now got yourself a genuine Go & Get It! Method Plan! Take one task at a time. It is also important to follow along with the sequential order of your plan as much as possible. Each task is a building block to get you to the next task.

There may be times where perhaps you are waiting on someone to get back to you or things might be on hold for other reasons. By all means, start in on other tasks that make sense to get done while you're in a holding pattern.

Stay Within Scope

Before you dive in to your tasks, I want to mention that it is always best to stick to the plan as best you can. As you begin to work through your plan, you may find other avenues cropping up that perhaps you hadn't thought of when you were initially filling out your sticky notes.

For example, for this book, I created a solid plan, but as time went on, I wanted to add additional features. I thought, wouldn't it be neat for the eBook version to have links that would take the reader to a quick video where I am explaining a particular topic? As much as I love this idea, it didn't work with my original plan. Doing it would mean it would take considerably longer for me to reach my immediate goal of publishing this book.

This doesn't mean I can't move forward on the video idea. I certainly hope to do so, but now is not the time. It takes discipline to stay the course and that is what you must do in order to successfully reach the finish line.

19 HOW DO YOU STAY MOTIVATED?

13. Stay Motivated

EVEN if you have all the passion in the world for what you're working on, sometimes it's tough to stay motivated. I can assure you taking each task one at a time and completing it will certainly give you a sense of satisfaction and the feeling you want to keep plugging.

Color Coding Shows Progress

As previously mentioned, when each task is complete, you should consider highlighting the row with a designated completion color, be it in an application or with a highlighter. It is so much fun watching as the plan becomes more and more colorful.

Remember Where You Were

Another way to stay motivated is to jot down where you want to jump back in on your work the next time you start up again. For example, let's say you've just had a very satisfying day trying out some new recording gear and the next step on your Go & Get It! Method Plan is to make a selection on what gear you'll go with.

All it will take is one sticky with the task of Make Selection of Gear written on it. Stick it on your desk, computer, coffee mug—anywhere you'll see it first thing when you start in on your plan again. This will immediately get you back on track.

If you work in an office, at the end of the day you should set aside a few minutes to get your bearings for the next day. Think of what you'll need to tackle first when you walk in and jot it down on a sticky. This will get you right on track in the morning from where you last left off.

Share

Let people know once in a while what you're up to. You don't have to go overboard with details. It should be just enough for them to be happy for you. What you should do is make really sure you don't let anyone keep you from your goal. It's bizarre, but sometimes when you're on a quest, others (sometimes even those you'd least expect) may not give you the encouragement you'd hope to have.

They may feel a bit jealous because something is keeping them from fulfilling their needs or wants. Don't take it personally and don't let it keep you from what you have to do. Just recognize it has nothing to do with you, and everything to do with them. Perhaps you'll find you have become an inspiration for them to get moving on their own dreams! Of course, you can always refer them to *You Want It? Then Damn It, Go & Get It!* Sorry, it's a shameless plug!

"It is not the critic who counts; not the man who points out how the strong man stumbles, or where the doer of deeds could have done them better. The credit belongs to the man who is actually in the arena, whose face is marred by dust and sweat and blood; who strives valiantly; who errs, who comes short again and again, because there is no effort without error and shortcoming; but who does actually strive to do the deeds; who knows great enthusiasms, the great

devotions; who spends himself in a worthy cause; who at the best knows in the end the triumph of high achievement, and who at the worst, if he fails, at least fails while daring greatly, so that his place shall never be with those cold and timid souls who neither know victory nor defeat."
– Theodore Roosevelt

Visualization

Remember when we chatted about visualization? Now is a good time to experiment with this technique to help you stay on track. Here are a few tips…

1. As you're first waking up in the morning or just about to fall asleep, take a few minutes to focus on your goal.

2. Close your eyes as you hold a mental picture of the goal in your mind. It should feel as though it is happening in the present moment.

3. Use all of your senses. For example, if you want to learn to sail, feel the boat beneath you in the waves. Smell the salt air. Hear the seagulls overhead. Feel the breeze blowing across your face. Feel the sheet in your hands as you're controlling the sail.

4. Get in touch with your feelings. Are you excited or exhilarated?

5. If you start to feel doubt at any time or begin to think what your striving for can't be achieved, recognize it and just mentally brush it away.

Practice makes perfect. You be the judge. Try this exercise and see if it helps. It can't hurt!

Do Not Procrastinate

Believe me, it will happen. No matter how excited you are about following your dreams, there will come a time where you avoid a task for one reason or another. Perhaps you're not sure of something and you're timid about finding out more. Here is my advice. DO NOT PUT IT OFF! Even if you have to take a little step toward it, just do so. Before you know it, you'll be moving through the motions and what you wanted to put off so badly is suddenly behind you. Procrastination brings nothing but delays, and why would you want to delay on turning your dreams into reality?

Resilience

I recently read a book, *Resilience* by Eric Greitens, which I highly recommend. Mr. Greitens is a former Navy Seal who now (among many other noble causes), helps veterans coming back from service to acclimate themselves back into the mainstream of society. Resilience means having the stamina to bounce back from difficulties. Here are just a few pointers, which resonated with me and may also help encourage you to stay the course.

1. *Hold Yourself Accountable* I'm betting that you often hold yourself accountable to others and their needs. How can you afford to give less to yourself than you do to others?

2. *Try Not To Lose Faith*
Mr. Greitens writes about the Stockdale Paradox. Its origin comes from Admiral James Stockdale who was a prisoner of war for 7 ½ years. Here is how Admiral Stockdale explains it: *"You must never confuse faith that you will prevail in the end—which you can never afford to lose—with discipline to confront the most brutal facts of your current reality, whatever they may be."* Hopefully you won't encounter a great deal of brutal facts of your current reality, but you may certainly come across roadblocks. The idea is to acknowledge the roadblock and somehow find a detour and have faith you will be able to get on a newly, paved road once again.

3. *Take It One Step At A Time*
   Eric Greiten offers some good advice, "Great changes come when we learn how to make small adjustments with great conviction. To get there, all you have to do right now is make a slight change of course. Point yourself in a new direction and start walking."

4. *You're Not Supposed To Know Everything*
   You may fail at things along the way, but if you have resilience, you'll be able to learn from the mistake and move on.

5. *You'll Always Find A Critic...*
   But don't let that stop you.
   I love this quote from Eleanor Roosevelt, "Do what you feel in your heart to be right—for you'll be criticized anyway. You'll be damned if you do, and

damned if you don't." So, Just Do It! as the Nike marketing slogan proclaims.

6. *Remember To Be Appreciative* As you go through the tasks at hand, remember to find time to feel gratitude. Remember, with each completed task, it's a win and something you should be grateful for.

20 HANG ON TO YOUR GO & GET IT! METHOD LIST & PLANS

AFTER finalizing my album, I was thrilled that all the hard and loving work that went into recording my music was complete. What I didn't mention earlier was that soon after its completion, I was suddenly inflicted with unexplained, severe muscle and joint pain, which left me incapacitated for over a year and a half. I was at a point where I couldn't even hold my guitar or get any farther than the end of my driveway when I was used to walking five miles several times a week. The marketing and promotion of my album had to be put on hold due to my health.

I shifted gears and used The Go & Get It! Method plan, which was a Godsend for me to keep track of my health, and the tasks I needed to perform to get back to where I needed to be. Just having a plan truly gave me a feeling of empowerment while facing the unknown.

After many blood tests and many doctor appointments with no answers, I was given prescription muscle relaxers for the pain. I fought this route and pursued other avenues on my own. I finally found relief and a long road back to health mainly through healthy eating (Preservatives, sugar, salt, etc., are causing havoc on our bodies, but that's got to be a topic for yet, another time.), acupuncture, meditation, prayer and yoga–thank you, Buddhaful Souls Yoga Studio (buddhafulsoulsyogastudio.com)!

I wanted my health back and damn it, I got it!

As we talked about earlier, attitude is everything. Keeping myself in the right frame of mind was crucial for me not to go off the emotional deep end. I didn't think of what happened yesterday or how long it would take to heal. I focused on the present and what I had to do to get healthy again. Sure, I freaked out once in awhile, especially without a confirmed diagnosis. I allowed myself to feel the fear, have a good cry, but I didn't let it take me into its clutches for very long. And I'm happy to say I'm back to health now!

Here's where the Go & Get It! Method Plan is helping out once again. Earlier in the book, I mentioned that you might not get to all the items on your Go & Get It! Method List. It's a live document. It can change due to your life circumstances and desires. There is nothing wrong with that. Just having it however, will always keep you on track of what you could pursue when you have the need or desire to do so. The Go & Get It! Method Plan works the same way. Would I have wanted to complete everything on the plan? Sure. Can I still do so for my album? Absolutely.

On the completion of this book, I have the luxury to go back and pick up on marketing for my album. I don't have to start from scratch. It's all there on the plan, waiting until I'm ready to go for it again. I won't beat myself up because other things got in the way for a while.

"Between stimulus and response, there is a space. In that space lays our freedom and power to choose our response. In our response lies our growth and freedom."

– Viktor E. Frankl, Man's Search for Meaning

Our time together is coming to a close for now. I invite you to look through the pages that follow. There you will find some resource material to help you stay on track. You'll also find a little more information on me, and some contact information. I would love to hear how you're doing!

I've really enjoyed this time together and I'm certain that if you really want it, well then damn it, you're going to get it! May all your dreams come true.

14. Reach Your Goals

###

APPENDIX
CHECKLISTS

WE certainly discussed a lot. I want to leave you with two checklists. The first is for figuring out what you'd like to pursue. If you've worked through the exercises in this book, you've already established a great Go & Get It! Method List. There may be times, however, where you might want to go back through the steps and review what you have. Remember, interests change over time and what you thought was important today may be very different a year from now.

The second checklist brings you through the steps once you've decided on the goal you've set for yourself, and you're ready to create your Go & Get It! Method Plan.

Next up is a chart that goes along with Chapter 9 Define What It Is.

And last are some definitions that you might find useful.

Checklist to Create Your Go & Get It! Method List

1. Make time for yourself

2. Find a place of comfort

3. Purchase your supplies

4. Get into the right frame of mind

5. Think what you want

6. Think what you need

6.1 Write each idea on a sticky

7. Arrange stickies in the order you want to proceed

8. Write out Go & Get It! Method List

Checklist to Create Your Go & Get It! Method Plan

1. Begin with the first item on your Go & Get It! Method List

2. Create mission statement

3. Write each action item on a sticky

4. Organize tasks sequentially within each bucket

5. Name your buckets

6. Organize your buckets sequentially

7. Find your resources

8. Recognize and appreciate your milestones

9. Think about a timeline

10. Decide where to lay out your information for your Go & Get It! Method Plan

11. Fill in your Go & Get It! Method Plan

- Buckets

- Sequential tasks

- Milestones

- Start date

- End date

- Resources

- Status

12. Start in on your tasks

13. Stay motivated

14. Reach your goals

To Be Used With Chapter 9 – Define What It Is

Emotion	Activity

Definitions

1. *Action Items:* Some type of documented task that needs to take place.

2. *Dependency:* Some type of action you have to take before you can go on to the next action.

3. *Gantt Chart:* A type of bar chart, developed by Henry Gantt, which illustrates a project schedule.

4. *Go & Get It! Method:* A process that identifies a goal and paves the way to reach that particular goal or intention.

5. *Go & Get It! Method List:* A list that contains the wants and needs you would like to pursue.

6. *Go & Get It! Method Plan:* A roadmap that outlines the defined process for an identified goal and paves the way to reach that particular goal or intention.

7. *Milestones:* Places you reach after all your tasks are complete from a particular bucket.

8. *Open Source Software:* Software whose code is available for changes or enhancements by anyone.

9. *PDF:* A portable document format, that preserves attributes of a source document no matter which application platform or hardware type was originally used to create it.

10. *Personal Productivity:* It uses a lot of the same methodology as project management, however, the individuals are now planning

and organizing, and securing, managing, leading and controlling resources for themselves and for the most part by themselves.

11. *Project:* An individual or collaborative, enterprise effort planned and designed to achieve a goal.

12. *Project Management:* Planning, organizing, securing, managing, leading, and controlling resources to achieve specific goals. This is typically done with a team of people.

13. *Roadmap:* A plan, which describes the means to connect vision, values, and objectives with strategic actions, that is required to achieve those objectives.

14. *Task:* A piece of work that needs to be done or undertaken.

15. *Time Management:* Being consciously aware of the time it takes to do a specific task.

About the Author

Renée Armand is: wife, proud mom, daughter, sister, friend, volunteer, musician, singer and songwriter, co-founder of SkyLight Creative, founder of The Passion to Pursue, author, happy redhead!

Renée Armand loves: family, friends, faith, lots of laughter, tea, guitar, reading, writing, making music, dancing, traveling, yoga, fire pits, wine & cats.

Renée Armand has been: cheerleader, non-profit worker, desktop publisher, teacher, manager of global group, project manager, world traveler, vice president in corporate US of A.

Photograph by: Diane O'Connor

Connect:

Music:
reneestcyr.com

The Passion To Pursue:
reneearmand.com

Twitter:
@reneearmand

Facebook:
facebook.com/ThePassionToPursue